Handwriting 5–6

Author: Stephanie Cooper
Illustrators: Emma Holt and Chris McGhie

How to use this book

Look out for these features!

IN THE ACTIVITIES
The parents' notes at the top of each activity will give you:
▶ a simple explanation about what your child is learning
▶ an idea of how you can work with your child on the activity.

This small page number guides you to the back of the book, where you will find further ideas for help.

These magic stars provide useful facts and helpful hints!

AT THE BACK OF THE BOOK
Every activity has a section for parents containing:
▶ further explanations about what the activity teaches
▶ games that can be easily recreated at home
▶ questions to ask your child to encourage their learning
▶ tips on varying the activity if it seems too easy or too difficult for your child.

You will also find the answers at the back of the book.

HELPING YOUR CHILD AS THEY USE THIS BOOK
Why not try starting at the beginning of the book and work through it? Your child should only attempt one activity at a time. Remember, it is best to learn little and often when we are feeling wide awake!

EQUIPMENT YOUR CHILD WILL NEED
▶ a pencil for writing
▶ an eraser for correcting mistakes
▶ coloured pencils for drawing and colouring in.

You might also like to have ready some spare paper and some collections of objects (for instance, small toys, Lego bricks, buttons...) for some of the activities.

Contents

Letters **4**

Beginning, middle and end **6**

ll words **8**

ss words **10**

Days of the week **12**

–n't endings **14**

–ck endings **16**

–nt endings **18**

ai words **20**

ee words **22**

ie words **24**

oa words **26**

u words **28**

–ld endings **30**

–nk and –lk endings **32**

–st endings **34**

–ng endings **36**

Three-letter endings **38**

More beginning, middle and end **40**

Make your own words **42**

Further activities **44**

Celebration! **48**

Letters

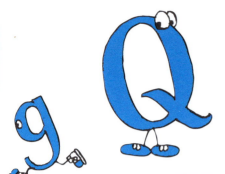
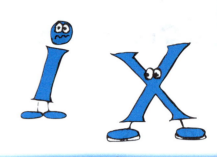

Copy out this alphabet.

a b c d e f g h i j k l m n

o p q r s t u v w x y z

Write the **vowels**.

__ __ __ __ __

These letters are all lower case.

> This activity will help you find out if your child knows all the alphabetic letter sounds and names.
> Ask them to say the name and sound of each letter.

Parents

44

Now try this one.

A B C D E F G H I J K L M

N O P Q R S T U V W X Y Z

Write the **consonants**.

___ ___ ___ ___ ___ ___ ___ ___

___ ___ ___ ___ ___ ___ ___ ___

___ ___ ___

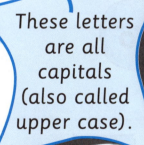

These letters are all capitals (also called upper case).

5

Beginning, middle and end

Choose the first, middle and last letters to write as many 3-letter words as you can.

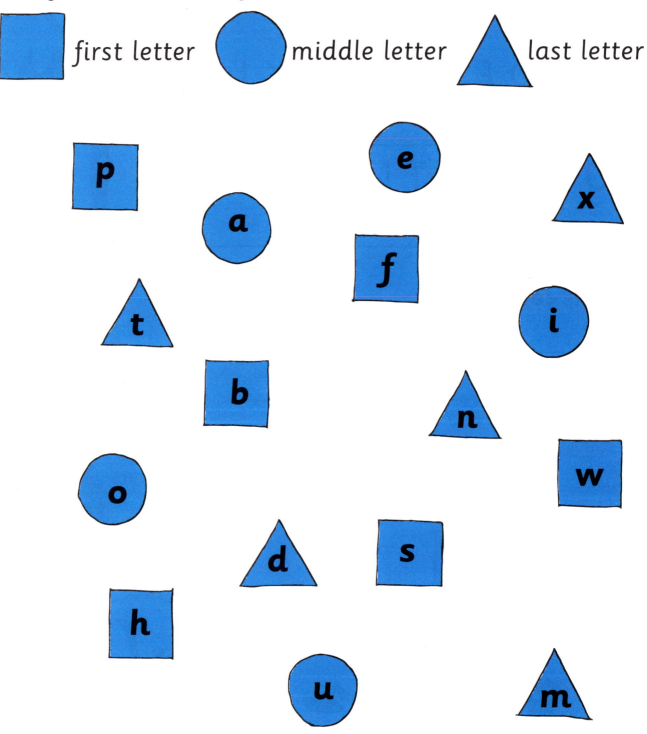

> This activity will help your child to learn to spell and write consonant-vowel-consonant words.

> Ask them to say if the words they write are real or not.

Parents

44

___ ___ ___

___ ___ ___

___ ___ ___

___ ___ ___

___ ___ ___

___ ___ ___

___ ___ ___

___ ___ ___

___ ___ ___

___ ___ ___

___ ___ ___

___ ___ ___

___ ___ ___

___ ___ ___

___ ___ ___

___ ___ ___

___ ___ ___

___ ___ ___

7

ll words

Practise writing these letters. _____

Now write these words.

1. football _____

2. ill _____

3. pill _____

4. thrill _____

5. fall _____

6. wall _____

> This activity will help your child to spell and write words ending in 'll' correctly.
>
> Make sure they know what each word says before writing it.

Parents

44

7. well _____

_____

8. bell _____

_____

9. skull _____

_____

10. hill _____

_____

11. smell _____

_____

12. dull _____

_____

9

ss words

Practise writing these letters. ss _____

Now write these words.

1. hiss _____

_____

2. class _____

_____

3. floss _____

_____

4. miss _____

_____

> This activity will help your child to learn how to write and spell correctly words ending with 'ss'.
>
> Make sure they write each 's' letter the right way round.

Parents

44

5. kiss _____

_____

6. Miss _____

_____

7. dress _____

_____

8. mess _____

_____

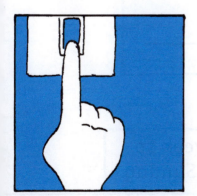

9. press _____

_____

11

Days of the week

List the days of the week.

Sunday

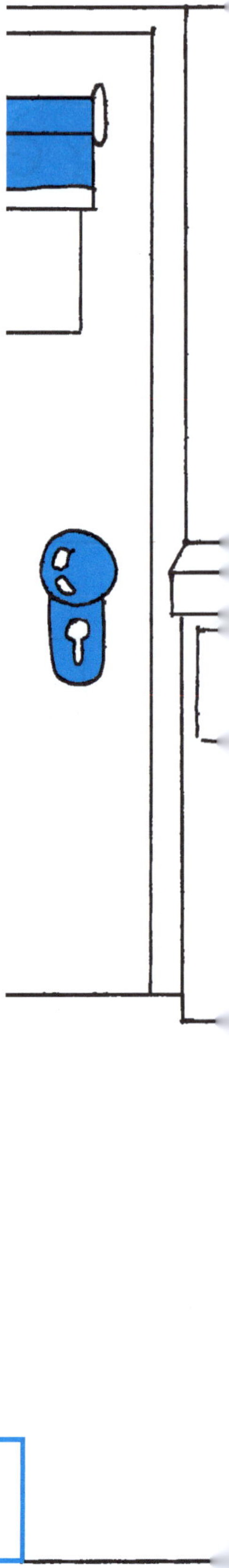

Circle all the words below with the **ay** sound.

Today is Monday. Help May's mum plan her week so that she is ready for May's birthday party on Sunday.

12

Parents

▶ This activity will help your child learn how to write and spell the days of the week correctly.

▶ Ask them to draw a circle around words they can see with the 'ay' sound.

44

Things to do by Sunday:

Monday – Make the birthday cake
Tuesday – Wash Jake and May
Wednesday – Decorate the birthday cake
Thursday – Buy May's birthday present
Friday – Lay the table
Saturday – Buy eight candles

–n't endings

Practise writing the words ending with **n't**.

do not = do+n~~o~~t = do**n't**

don't: _____

will not = wi~~ll~~+n~~o~~t = wo**n't**

won't: _____

can not = can+no̸t = ca**n't**

can't: _____

did not = did+no̸t = did**n't**

didn't: _____

15

–ck endings

Practise writing these letters. ck _____

Now write these words.

1. tick tock _____

_____

2. sock _____

_____

3. clock _____

_____

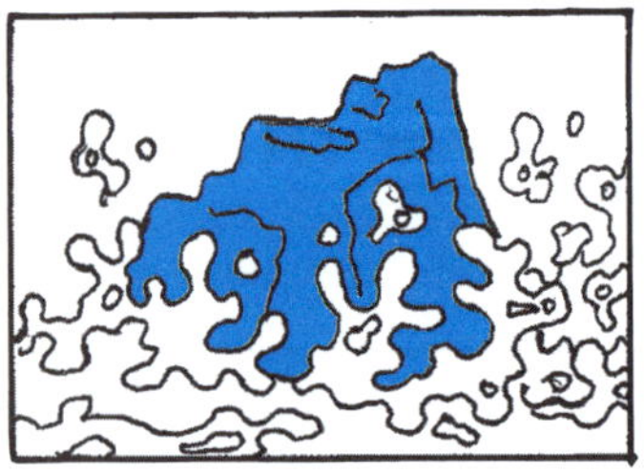

4. rock _____

_____

5. duck _____

_____

6. truck _____

_____

> This activity will help your child to learn how to write and spell correctly words ending in 'ck'.
>
> Ask them to read all the words on the page first, using the pictures to help them.

45

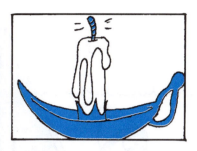

7. wick _____

_____

8. lick _____

_____

9. click _____

_____

10. shock _____

_____

11. trick _____

_____

12. luck _____

_____

–nt endings

> **Parents**
>
> ▶ This activity will help your child to learn how to write and spell correctly words ending 'nt'.
> ▶ Watch for 'b'/'d' reversal when your child is writing 'bent' and 'dent'.
>
> 45

Write a list of all the words and objects in the picture that end with **nt**.

nt _____

nt words

19

ai words

Read these sentences. Circle the **ay** words

1. Trains go fast.
2. Children play.
3. Horses eat hay.
4. My birthday is in May.
5. I hate to drink coffee.
6. Look! It's a plane!
7. My mum is great.

Practise writing these.

ay	ea	a_e	ai
___	___	___	___

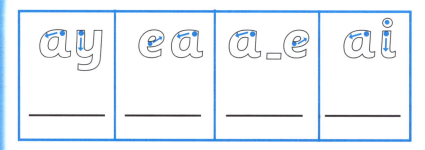

> This activity will help your child learn words with the letters 'ai', 'ea', 'a_e' and 'ay' which make the 'ay' sound.
> Circle the 'ay' words with your child first.

Now write the words which have an **ai** sound in them.

ay _____

_____

ea _____

_____

a_e _____

_____

ai _____

_____

ee words

Read these sentences. Circle the **ee** words.

1. Mice squeak.

2. I speak.

3. Chicks cheep.

4. Birds tweet.

5. I am asleep.

6. I am up a tree.

7. Lambs bleat.

8. We are free.

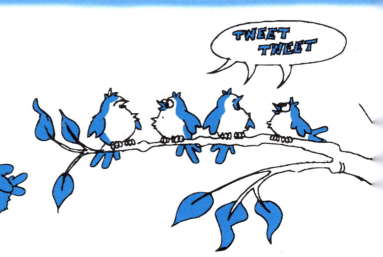

▶ This activity will help your child to learn words with 'ee' and 'ea' letters which make the 'ee' sound.
▶ Circle the 'ee' words in each sentence with your child first.

Parents

45

Practise writing these.

ee _____

_____

ea _____

_____

23

ie words

Read these sentences. Circle the words with the **i** sound.

1. My dad is nice.
2. I love eating pies.
3. Birds fly high.
4. Sharks bite.
5. Planes fly in the sky.
6. The night is dark.
7. The knight is brave.

Practise these.

i_e	igh	y	ie
___	___	___	___

▶ This activity will help your child learn words with 'y', 'igh', 'ie' and 'i_e' letters which make the 'i' sound.
▶ Ask your child to circle the 'ie' words first.

Parents

46

Now list the **i** sound words here.

i_e _____

_____

igh _____

_____

y _____

_____

ie _____

_____

'ie', 'y', and 'igh' all make the 'i' sound.

oa words

Read these sentences. Circle the words with the **oa** words.

1. Toads croak.
2. Whales blow.
3. Deep snow.
4. Boats float.
5. Jo went home.
6. Warm coat.
7. No sweets.

Practise the letters here.

oa	o_e	ow	o
___	___	___	___

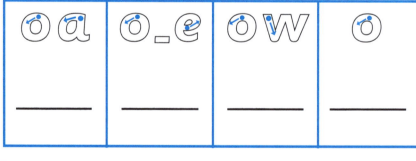

Parents

▶ This activity will help your child to learn words with 'oa', 'o_e', 'o' and 'ow' letters which make the 'o' sound.
▶ Ask your child to point to these sounds in each sentence first.

46

Now list the words with an **oa** sound.

oa _____

_____

o_e _____

_____

ow _____

_____

o _____

_____

u words

Read these sentences. Circle the words with a **u** sound.

1. You are huge.
2. Miss Pew knew.
3. New tune.
4. Crocodile stew.
5. New dress.
6. Ewes leap.
7. Tube of toothpaste.

Practise these spellings.

ew	u	u_e
___	___	___

28

> This activity will help your child to learn words with 'ew', 'u', and 'u_e' letters which make the 'u' sound.
> Ask your child to circle the 'u' words first.

Parents

46

Now list the words with a **u** sound.

ew _____

_____

u _____

_____

u_e _____

_____

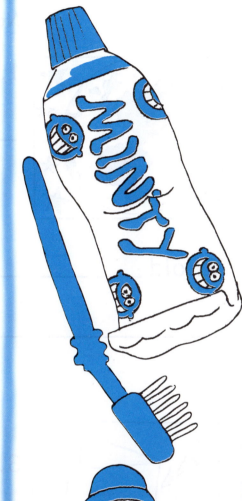

−ld endings

Practise writing these letters.

Now write these words.

1. world _____

   _____

2. old _____

   _____

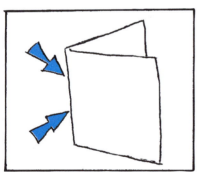

3. fold _____

   _____

4. cold _____

   _____

> This activity will help your child to learn how to write and spell correctly words ending '-ld'.
> Ask them to find and point to the 'ld' sound in each word.

Parents

46

5. bald _____

   _____

6. gold _____

   _____

7. mould _____

   _____

8. sold _____

   _____

9. told _____

   _____

31

–nk and –lk endings

Practise writing these letters. nk _____

Now write a sentence for each picture.
Do it like this.

1. blink _____

The girl is blinking. _____

2. think _____

_____

3. wink_____

_____

4. stink_____

_____

5. tank _____

_____

6. pink_____

_____

> **Parents**
>
> ▶ This activity will help your child to learn how to write and spell correctly words ending '-lk' and '-nk'.
>
> ▶ Ask your child to write a sentence to go with each picture using an '-nk' or '-lk' word, showing them how to spell it first.
>
> 46

7. bunk _____

_____

8. bank _____

_____

lk _____

9. walk _____

The 'l' in these words is silent.

_____

10. talk _____

_____

33

–st endings

> **Parents** 47
>
> ▶ This activity will help your child to learn how to write and spell correctly words ending in '-st'.
> ▶ Ask your child to look for objects in the picture that end in '-st'.

Look for the words and objects that end with the letters **st** in the picture. Then practice writing them here.

st_____

st words

_____
_____
_____
_____
_____
_____
_____
_____

35

–ng endings

Practise writing these letters.

Now put these words in a sentence.

1. song _____

   _____

2. ding dong _____

   _____

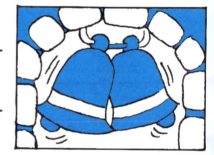

3. bang _____

   _____

4. wrong _____

   _____

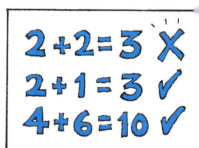

5. ring _____

   _____

36

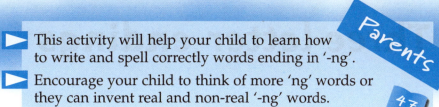

▶ This activity will help your child to learn how to write and spell correctly words ending in '-ng'.

▶ Encourage your child to think of more 'ng' words or they can invent real and non-real '-ng' words.

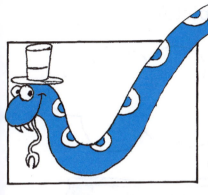

6. long _____

_____

7. king _____

_____

8. string _____

_____

9. wing _____

_____

10. cling _____

_____

Three-letter endings

Look for the words that end with **nch** in the picture.

38

> This activity will help your child learn how to write and spell correctly words ending in '-nch'.
>
> Ask your child to look for objects in the picture that end in '-nch'.

Parents

47

Practise writing these letters.

nch _____

Now list all the **nch** words and objects in the picture.

_____

_____

_____

_____

_____

_____

_____

_____

39

More beginning, middle and end

thri _ _

sku _ _

Choose a beginning, a middle and an end to make as many words as you can.

- ◼ first letter
- ● middle letter
- ▲ last letter

o, thr, b, ss, ck, e, br, cr, t, ng, nch, sk, tr, m, sh, bl, ll, a, u, nk, fl, i

cra _ _

sho _ _

cru _ _ _

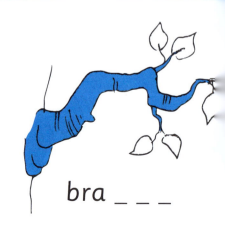

bra _ _ _

40

trick

▶ This activity will help your child to learn how to spell and write words ending in '-ck', '-ll', '-nch', '-nt', '-ss' '-nk' and '-ng' independently.
▶ They can complete and use the clues in the border to help them.

Do it like this:
tr + i + ck = trick

ba _ _

te _ _

me _ _

flo _ _

bli _ _

Make your own words

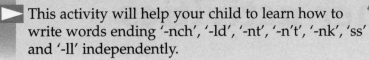

Parents

- This activity will help your child to learn how to write words ending '-nch', '-ld', '-nt', '-n't', '-nk', 'ss' and '-ll' independently.
- Encourage them to use other pages in the book for ideas.

Write some real words that the word machine can make.

nch　ld　nt　n't　nk　ck　ss　ll

Further activities

4–5

▶ If your child doesn't yet know all the letter sounds and names, work on them now. Make some simple 3-letter words together, for example, 'dog', 'map', 'mug', 'wet' and 'big', and split the word into three so they can hear each sound of each letter, such as 'd–o–g'. Then write down the first and the last letter in a word and ask them to write in the missing middle letter, for example,

'w_t' (wet). The middle sound is harder to hear than the first or the last.

▶ To broaden this, ask them to write down simple words as you dictate them. Say one word at a time and give them plenty of time to think before they write.

▶ *Answers: vowels: a, e, i, o, u; consonants: b, c, d, f, g, h, j, k, l, m, n, p, q, r, s, t, v, w, x, y, z.*

6–7

▶ Make sure your child is forming each of the letters correctly at this stage. If they are not, show them how. Then ask them to write more consonant-vowel-consonant words, for example, 'lid' or 'not'.

▶ Ask them to write 3-letter words that rhyme, for

example, words that rhyme with 'Ben' (hen, pen, ten, nen – it doesn't matter if they are real words or not).

▶ *Answers: Some examples are put, sun, bed, fun, ham, pot, pod, bad, fox, box, fix, fit, had, sad, sat, sit, hum, hid... and there are many more.*

8–9

▶ Ask your child to think of more words with an '-ll' ending. Talk about words that end with an 'l' sound, but which are not spelled with a double 'l', for example, 'bowl'.

▶ When your child is practising how to write a word, make sure they know what the word is and that they are not just blindly copying. When they

are familiar with these words, show them how to write the 'll' ending, then each word, in a cursive style.

ll   football   wall

... and so on.

10–11

▶ If your child writes 's' the wrong way round often, ask them to write the letter with you in a tray of sand or salt, then to try again on paper. Make sure they learn how to write it correctly now, so that they feel confident about writing independently.

▶ Point out that some words ending with the 's'

sound only have one 's' at the end, for example, 'bus', 'Chris', 'us'.

▶ When your child is familiar with these words, show them how to write the 'ss' ending, then each word, in a cursive style.

ss   class   Miss

12–13

▶ Talk about other words on the page which have an 'a' sound, for example, 'Jake', 'make', 'cake', 'lay', 'decorate', 'eight', 'Fay', 'May', 'birthday'. Ask your child to practise writing these words.

▶ Show your child how to write the days of the week as an abbreviation (Mon, Tue, Wed, Thur, Fri, Sat, Sun). When they are familiar with

writing the days of the week, practise writing them in a cursive style.

▶ *Answers: Monday, Tuesday, Wednesday, Thursday, Friday, Saturday.*
ay words – Today, Monday, May, birthday, Sunday.

15

▶ Encourage your child to use words with and without apostrophes in independent writing, for example, 'can', 'can't' and 'can not', so that they remember how to write and spell both versions.

▶ When your child is familiar with writing these words, introduce them to the cursive style.

*don't won't
didn't can't*

▶ *Answers: don't, won't, can't, didn't.*

17

▶ Ask your child to think of other words that end with 'ck', for example, 'luck', 'thick', 'brick', 'cluck'. Ask them to write sentences which include two or more words ending in 'ck', for example, 'The clock went tick tock'. Make sure they spell any 'ck' words they use correctly.

▶ Suggest they write a story which includes ten different 'ck' words that you give them to reinforce this letter recognition.

19

▶ Ask your child to write other words ending in 'nt', for example, 'aunt', 'went', 'lent'.

▶ To extend this further, ask them to write their own sentences about each 'nt' word they know, to make sure they understand what each word means. For example, 'My auntie Jane lent me her Lion King video'.

▶ When your child is familiar with writing these words, introduce them to the cursive style.

▶ *Answers: want, can't, dent, front, bent, didn't, ant, tent, Kent.
Answers may vary.*

21

▶ Make sure you pronounce these words 'ay' rather than saying the sound of each separate letter.

▶ Ask your child to think of some words that rhyme with 'play' ('ray' and 'way'), to think of words that rhyme with 'train' ('rain' and 'grain') and to think of words with an a_e 'ay' sound ('blame' and 'shape'). Spend some time with this, because it is a tricky sound for children to learn.

▶ If your child has a word book, write each of these words into it so that they can turn to them independently.

▶ *Answers: 'ay' words: play, hay, birthday, May; 'ea' words: eat, great; 'a_e' words: hate, plane; 'ai' word: trains.*

23

▶ Pronounce the underlined parts of these words with the 'ee' sound rather than pronouncing the separate letters on their own.

▶ Ask your child to think of other 'ee' and 'ea' words, for example, 'seat', 'sweet', 'need' and 'feet', and to practise writing them. Introduce the cursive style of writing 'ee' and 'ea' once your child is familiar with them.

ee ea

▶ *Answers: 'ee' words: cheep, tweet, asleep, tree, free; 'ea' words: squeak, speak, bleat.*

45

Further activities

▶ Say the underlined parts of these words with the 'i' sound rather than pronouncing the separate letters on their own. Write a list of 'i_e' words together, and ask your child to practise writing them ('spice', 'rice', 'ice'.) Then ask them to write each word into a sentence.

▶ To extend this further, ask your child to use a list of words to try to write their own poem. Write one together first, before they try on their own.

▶ Check through their writing to make sure that the 'ie' words they use are spelled and written correctly.

▶ *Answers: 'i_e' words: nice, bite; 'igh' words: high, night, knight; 'y' words: fly, sky; 'ie' word: pies.*

▶ Say these words with the 'o' sound rather than pronouncing the separate letters on their own.

▶ Write a list of 'ow' words together, for example, 'know' and 'row'. Ask your child to think of some more 'ow' words, real or imagined ('tow' and 'zow'), and to practise writing them.

Then ask them to write the real words into a sentence, to give them meaning.

▶ *Answers: 'oa' words: toads, croak, boats, float, coat; 'o_e' words: home; 'ow' words: blow, snow; 'o' words: Jo, no.*

▶ Pronounce the underlined parts of these words with the 'u' sound rather than pronouncing the separate letters on their own. Make sure your child recognises the difference between the sound in 'moon' and 'tooth'.

▶ When your child practises handwriting, make sure they form each letter correctly, but let them enjoy handwriting on their own, too. Introduce a cursive style once they are familiar with the sounds.

▶ *Answers: 'ew' words: pew, knew, new, stew, ewes; 'u' words: you; 'u_e' words: tune, huge, tube.*

▶ Reinforce this activity by asking your child to write a story about an old bald man called Ronald, who travelled to the other side of the world to find a bag of gold. Ask them to include as many words with '-ld' endings in the story as they can. Make a list with them first, to give them some ideas.

▶ Introduce a cursive style of writing once your child is familiar with the sound.

▶ Pronounce the '-nk' ending as one sound rather than saying each letter sound separately. And pronounce the '-lk' ending 'awk', to make it easier for your child to hear in the context of the words.

▶ To extend this activity further, ask your child to practise writing words with 'nk' in the middle, for example, 'thinking' or 'winking'.

▶ Introduce a cursive style of writing once your child is familiar with the sounds.

46

▶ Ask your child to write a list of other words ending in '-st' ('blast', 'last' and 'must').

▶ Develop this further by looking together at words which begin with 'st', for example, 'stop', 'start', 'stare'. Then discuss words that have 'st' in the middle, for example, 'postman' and 'poster' so they have experience at listening to the same 'st' sound in different parts of a word.

▶ *Answers: toast, mist, ghost, lost, list, post, first. Answers may vary.*

▶ Ask your child to practise writing a list of words with 'ng' in the middle, for example, 'singing', 'ringing', 'bringing' and 'tongue'.

▶ Write the words for them first, so they learn how to write each one in the correct way. Ask them to highlight the 'ng' part of each word.

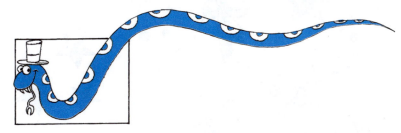

▶ Encourage your child to identify other word endings, including, '-mp', '-sp', '-ct', '-ft', '-lt', '-pt' and '-lf'.

Only introduce your child to a new word ending every few days, or one each week, to avoid confusion. Ask them to write each ending on its own, then to write it in the context of a word.

▶ Then look for words with the same ending in a story, reference book or dictionary. Always write new words into your child's word book, so that they can use them when they are writing independently.

▶ *Answers: bunch, lunch, munch, crunch, branch, trench, bench. Answers may vary.*

▶ Ask your child to make as many words as they can. Here are some ideas: 'trick', 'skull', 'shock', 'crunch', 'branch', 'thrill', 'crack', 'bang', 'tent', 'blink', 'floss', 'mess', 'track', 'back', 'bent', 'shell', 'tell', 'shall', 'bill', 'mint'.

▶ To extend this activity, write these letters on square-, circle- and triangle-shaped cards, then ask your child to make each word.

Develop this idea by adding or replacing one of the beginnings or endings.

▶ *Answers: There are many possible answers.*

▶ Ask your child to make as many real or imaginary words as they can – here are some ideas: 'tonk', 'clunch', 'lunch', 'flick', 'hill', 'wiss', 'fold', 'can't', 'ant', 'bank'… and there are plenty more.

▶ Write each word your child can think of on a card, then ask them to sort the words out, putting the '-nch' words together, and so on. Then to sort them into real and imaginary words.

47

Celebration!

You are so clever! Colour the stars to show what you can do!

I can write five words ending in st.

I can write five words ending in ng.

I can write five words ending in nch.

I can write five words ending in ll and ss.